CAITLIN
MORAN

How To Be A
Woman

EBURY
PRESS

1

This Quick Reads edition published in 2021 by Ebury Press,
an imprint of Ebury Publishing.

First published by Ebury Press in 2011

20 Vauxhall Bridge Road
London SW1V 2SA

Ebury Press is part of the Penguin Random House group
of companies whose addresses can be found at
global.penguinrandomhouse.com

Penguin
Random House
UK

www.penguin.co.uk

A CIP catalogue record for this book is available from the British
Library

ISBN 9781529109092

Typeset in 12 pt/16 pt ITC Stone Serif Std
by Integra Software Services Pvt. Ltd, Pondicherry

Printed and bound in Great Britain by Clays Ltd, Elcograf S.p.A.

The author and publisher are committed to the Penguin Random House
Ireland, Morrison Chambers, 32 Nassau Street, Dublin D02 YH68.

Penguin Random House is committed to a sustainable future for
our business, our readers and our planet. This book is made from

Contents

CONTENTS

Prologue

The Worst Birthday Ever

WOLVERHAMPTON, 5 APRIL 1988

I am running. I am running from The Yobs.
  'Boy!'
  'Gyppo!'
  'Boy!'
  I'm running from The Yobs in the playground by our house. I've seen nature films like this. I can see what's happening. I am 'the weak antelope, apart from the pack'. They are 'the lions'. They don't like my 'look' – Wellie boots, NHS glasses, and my dad's coat. I do not look very feminine. Kylie Minogue looks feminine.
  'Pikey!'
  The Yobs pause, to throw gravel at me.
  'You bloke! You – *bummer!*'

Back home, after I've finished crying, I write in my diary. Today is also my thirteenth birthday

– happy birthday to me! – and I like to be cheerful in my entries.

'My 13th birthday!!!!' I write in my diary. 'Porridge for brekkie, sausage and chips for dinner, baguette for tea. Got £20 all in all. 4 cards and 2 letters. Get green (teenage) ticket from library tomorrow!!!!! Man next door asked us if we wanted some chairs he was throwing out. We said YES!!!!'

I stare at the entry for a minute. I should put everything in, I think. I can't leave out the bad stuff.

'Some boys were shouting rude things in the field,' I write, slowly. 'It is because their willies are getting big.'

I have read enough to know that sexual desires can often make teenage boys act cruelly towards girls. I *also* know it wasn't *really* desire that made those boys throw gravel at me while I ran up a hill – but I don't want my diary to pity me. As far as my diary will know, I had the upper hand there. This diary is for glory only.

I stare at the entry. A moment of truth washes over me. Here I am, sharing my bed with a toddler, and wearing my dad's old thermal underwear as pyjamas. I am thirteen years old, I am 13 stone, I have no money, no friends, and

DUDLEY PUBLIC LIBRARIES

The loan of this book may be renewed if not required by other readers, by contacting the library from which it was borrowed.

cult. From mental health to social mobility, reading has a proven positive impact on life's big challenges. Find out more:

reading

#Quick

Books By Caitlin Moran

Non-fiction

How To Be A Woman
Moranthology
Moranifesto
More Than A Woman
Are Men Obsolete? (co-author)

Fiction

How To Build A Girl
How To Be Famous

boys throw gravel at me when they see me. It is my birthday, and I went to bed at 7.15 p.m.

I turn to the back page of my diary. This is where I have my 'long-term' projects.

For instance, 'My Bad Points'.

My Bad Points

1) I eat too much
2) I don't exercise
3) Quick bursts of rage
4) Losing everything

'My Bad Points' were written down on New Year's Eve. A month later, I have written my progress report:

1) I no longer eat ginger nuts
2) Take dog for a walk every day
3) Trying
4) Trying

Underneath all these, I draw a line, and write my new list.

By the Time I'm 18
1) Lose weight
2) Have good clothes

3) Have friends
4) Train dog properly
5) Ears pierced?

Oh God. I don't have a clue. I don't have a clue how I will ever be a woman.

In the thirty-two years since my thirteenth birthday, I have become far more positive about being a woman. To be honest, things picked up a lot when I got some fake ID, a laptop and a nice blouse. But in many ways, there is no worse present to give a child than hormones and a big pair of tits. Had anyone asked me before my birthday, I would have asked for a book token, or maybe a voucher for Topshop, instead.

Becoming a woman felt a bit like becoming famous. Instead of being ignored, a teenage girl is suddenly interesting to others, and gets hit with questions:

What size are you?
Have you done it yet?
Will you have sex with me?
Have you got ID?
Do you want to try a puff of this?
Are you seeing anyone?
Have you got protection?
What's your 'signature style'?

Can you walk in heels?
Who are your heroes?
Are you getting a Brazilian?
What porn do you like?
Do you want to get married?
When are you going to have kids?
Are you a feminist?
Were you just flirting with that man?
What do you want to do?
WHO ARE YOU?

All stupid questions to ask of a thirteen-year-old simply because she now needs a bra. They might as well have been asking my dog. I had no idea.

How To Be a Woman is the story of all the times that I got being a woman wrong. I don't know if we can talk about 'waves' of feminism any more – but I think the next wave would be the fifth.

If there is to be a fifth wave of feminism, I hope that women deal with the trouble and bullshit of being a modern woman in a new way. I hope that they don't shout at it, bottle it up inside them or argue with each other about it. I hope that they simply point at it, and go 'HA!', instead.

If there is a fifth wave, then this is my part of it. A book about how I had no idea of how to be a woman.

Chapter 1

I Start Bleeding!
And Become Furry!

I know that women bleed every month, but I did not think it was going to happen to *me*. I had thought I would just be able to ... opt out of it. It doesn't look that much use, or fun. I am just ... not going to bother! I think to myself, cheerfully, as I do my ten sit-ups a night. Captain Moran is opting out!

I had only found out about periods four months ago, anyway. My mother never told us about them – 'I thought you had picked it all up from *Moonlighting*,' she said when I asked her about it. It was only when I found a Lil-Lets leaflet stuffed in the hedge outside our house that I found out what the whole periods deal was.

'I don't want to talk about this,' my sister Caz says, when I try to show the leaflet to her.

'But have you seen?' I ask her, sitting on the end of her bed. 'Look – this is the *womb,* and this is *the vagina,* and the Lil-Let expands to fill the ... *burrow,*' I say. I've only skim-read the leaflet. To be honest, it has blown my mind quite badly. 'And it says it happens *every month,*' I say, to Caz.

Caz is now lying, fully dressed, under her duvet, wearing Wellie boots. 'I want you to go away,' her voice says, from under the duvet. 'I am pretending you're dead. I can't think of anything I want to do less than talk about periods with you.'

'I'm going to talk to Mum.'

I track Mum down on the toilet. She's eight-months pregnant, and holding the sleeping one-year-old Cheryl while trying to do a wee. I sit on the edge of the bath.

'Mum?' I say. For some reason, I think I am allowed only one question about periods. One shot at the 'period chat'.

'Yes?' she answers. Even though she is doing a wee and holding a sleeping baby, she is also sorting out a whites wash from the washing basket.

'You know – my period?' I whisper.

'Yes?' she says.

'Will it hurt?' I ask.

Mum thinks for a moment. 'Yeah,' she says, in the end. 'But it's OK.'

The baby then starts crying, so she never explains why it's 'OK'.

Three weeks later, my period starts. It is a deeply gloomy event. It starts in the car on the way to Central Library in town. I have to walk around the Non-Fiction section for half an hour, really hoping it won't show. Then Dad takes us all home again.

'My first period started: yuk,' I write in my diary.

The bag of sanitary towels my mum keeps on the back of the bathroom door has become *my* business now, too. I feel a sad envy of all my younger siblings who are still 'outside the bag'. The towels are thick, and cheap. Stuck into my pants, they feel like a mattress between my legs.

'It feels like a mattress between my legs,' I tell Caz. 'A horrible, thick mattress,' I go on. 'Like in *The Princess and the Pea*.'

Because the sanitary towels are cheap, they shred between my legs when I walk, and become useless and leaky. I give up walking for the rest of my period.

My first period lasts three months. I think this is perfectly normal. I faint quite often. I become so weak that my finger- and toenails become very pale blue.

I don't tell Mum – because I've asked my question about periods. Now I just have to … *get on with them.*

The blood on the sheets is grim – not dramatic, and red, like a murder, but brown, and boring, like an accident. It looks like I am rusty inside and am now breaking.

To avoid washing stains out every morning, I stuff huge bundles of loo roll in my pants, along with the useless sanitary towel. And I lie very, very still all night. Sometimes, there are huge blood clots, that look like raw liver. I guess this is the lining of my womb, coming off in inch-thick slices.

It all adds to a sense that something wrong is going on but that it is against the rules of the game to ever mention it.

I think about all the women through history, who've had to deal with this bullshit with just rags and cold water. No wonder women have been oppressed by men for so long, I think as I scrub my pants with a toothbrush. Getting dried blood out of cotton is a bitch. We women were all too busy doing laundry to fight for the vote until the twin-tub was invented.

*

Our house is cold – cold and small. When you get out of the bath, you wrap yourself in a damp towel, and run downstairs to dry in front of the fire.

It's Saturday night, so the TV is on. The sofa has six people on it, of varying sizes, packed in tight. Some people are lying on top of other people.

I come into the room and crouch in front of the fire. I still have the shower cap on, which is one of the best things in our house. It's one of our more feminine items. I always feel a little bit girly wearing it. I start to put on my nightie.

'Oooooooh!' rings out a voice, suddenly, from the sofa. It's my mother. 'Is that PUBES I can see? PUBES, Cate?'

Hair is one of the first worries of being a woman. It just appears and you must decide what to do about it. Hair is the first round in decades of quietly screaming 'WHO AM I?' while standing in Boots, clutching an empty basket. Shave or wax it off – or not?

In recent years I have had stronger and stronger opinions about pubic hair. I've got to the point where I now believe that there are only four things a grown, modern woman should have:

a pair of yellow shoes (they go with
   everything)

a friend who will come and post bail at
  4 a.m.
a fail-safe pie recipe
and a proper muff. A big, hairy minge.

I am aware that my views on waxing go against current thinking. But I can't believe we've got to a point where it's costing us *money* to have a fanny. All that hair-removal – it costs *a lot.*

They're basically making us pay for upkeep of our minges – like they're a shared garden. It's a stealth tax. Fanny VAT. This is money we should be spending on THE ELECTRICITY BILL and CHEESE and HATS. Instead, we're wasting it on making our fanny look like a skanky chicken breast from Lidl.

Given that it is simply a 'porn thing' – for this is where the trend for fully-waxed fannies began – our support for the idea is bizarre. Ladies! This shit doesn't apply to us! *We're* not getting paid for this! *Our* fannies aren't being viewed by millions! We don't need to bother!

But, of course, it *does* apply to us, as I've said. Because hardcore porn is now the main form of sex education in the Western world. This is where teenage boys and girls are 'learning' what to do to each other, and what to expect when they take each other's clothes off.

If you listen to conversations on the back row of the bus, you can hear fourteen-year-old boys being horrified to discover that, on fingering a thirteen-year-old girl, she has pubic hair. It makes me sad that thirteen-year-old girls are spending what little money they have on getting their foofs stripped. They should be spending that money on the really important stuff:

hair dye
tights
Jilly Cooper paperbacks
the Guns N' Roses back catalogue
the poems of Larkin
KitKats
Thunderbird 22
earrings that make your ears go green and
  septic
train tickets as far away from your
  hometown as you can possibly afford.

TAKE YOUR BIG FURRY MINGE TO DUBLIN, that's what I say.

Because there is a great deal of pleasure to be had in a proper, furry muff. So yeah. Keep it trimmed, keep it neat, but keep it as it's supposed to be: an old-school, born-to-rule, hot, right, grown woman's muff.

Chapter 2

I Am A Feminist!

What is feminism? It is the belief that women should be as free as men.

I was fifteen when I first said, 'I am a feminist.'

Here I am in my bedroom, saying it. I am looking in the mirror, watching myself say it: 'I am a feminist. I am a feminist.'

It is three years since I wrote my 'Things To Do By The Time I Am 18' list, and I am slowly making a plan of who I should be. I still haven't got my ears pierced, lost any weight or trained the dog, and all my clothes are still awful.

Then, I find Germaine Greer – maybe the most feminist person on TV. She uses the words 'liberation' and 'feminism', and I realise that she is the first person I've ever seen who doesn't say them as a joke. She says 'I am a feminist' in a perfectly calm way. It sounds like the answer to a puzzle that's been going on for years.

8

Greer says it with pride: the word is a prize that billions of women, for the span of human history, fought to win.

In later years, I would start to disagree with Greer on things that she said. But at fifteen, I am so excited about being a woman that, had I been a boy, I think I would have switched sides. In 1990, at fifteen-and-a-half, I am walking around saying, 'I'm a feminist,' in the same way normal people are going round saying, 'Loadsa money!', 'Rodney, you plonker' or 'Follow the bear!' I have discovered part of who I am.

Of course, you might be asking yourself, 'Am *I* a feminist? I might not be. I don't know! I still don't know what it is! I'm too tired and confused to work it out. I don't have time to decide about women's liberation! There seems to be a lot to it. WHAT DOES IT MEAN?'

I understand. So here is the quick way of working out if you're a feminist. Put your hand in your pants. a) Do you have a vagina? and b) Do you want to be in charge of it? If you said 'yes' to both, then well done! You're a feminist.

Now, what I am going to ask you to do is say, 'I am a feminist'. Say it out loud. In fact, I would like you to *stand on a chair,* and shout, 'I AM A FEMINIST.' Anything is more exciting if you stand on a chair to do it.

It really is important you say those words out loud. 'I AM A FEMINIST.'

If you feel you cannot say it – not even standing on the ground – I would be worried. It's probably one of the most important things a woman will ever say. The equal of 'I love you', 'Is it a boy or a girl?' or 'No! I've changed my mind! Do NOT cut me a fringe!'

Say it. SAY IT! SAY IT NOW! Because if you can't, you're basically bending over, saying, 'Kick my arse and take my vote, please, men.'

And do not think you shouldn't be standing on that chair, shouting 'I AM A FEMINIST!' if you are a boy. A male feminist should ABSOLUTELY be on the chair – so we ladies may all toast you, in champagne. And maybe you can change that light bulb, while you're up there. We cannot do it ourselves. There is a big spider's web on the fitting.

Because we need to reclaim the word 'feminism'. Only 29 per cent of American women and 42 per cent of British women describe themselves as feminist. This used to make me think, What do you think feminism IS, ladies? What part of 'liberation for women' is not for you? Is it freedom to vote? The right not to be owned by the man you marry? The campaign for equal pay? 'Vogue', by Madonna? Jeans? Did all that good shit GET ON YOUR NERVES? Or were you just DRUNK BACK THEN?

These days, I am much calmer – since I saw that it's basically impossible for a woman to argue against feminism. Without feminism, you wouldn't be allowed to have a debate on a woman's place in the world in the first place. You'd be too busy giving birth on the kitchen floor before going back to cleaning the toilet.

This is why those female writers in the *Daily Mail*, saying they hate feminism, amuse me. They paid you £1,600 to write that, dear, I think. And I bet the money is going in your bank account – not your husband's. The 'What I'm Really Thinking' bit in *The Guardian* ran the secret thoughts of a cleaner: 'Sometimes I think about the weird parts of the job: for example, that all the ironing is of men's clothing. To escape household chores, women won't iron their husband's shirts. Congratulations: your act of feminism means that the job is shunted onto a different woman, giving her a different rank.'

I've seen this idea a hundred times – that a proper feminist would do her own hoovering. Can you hire a cleaner and be a feminist?

But, of course, hiring a cleaner isn't a case of women oppressing other women, because:

WOMEN DID NOT INVENT DUST.
THE STICKY MESS THAT COLLECTS ON
THE KETTLE DOES NOT COME OUT OF
WOMEN'S VAGINAS.
IT IS NOT HORMONES THAT COVER
THE DINNER PLATES IN TOMATO SAUCE,
FISH-FINGER CRUMBS AND BITS OF MASH.
MY WOMB DID NOT RUN UPSTAIRS
AND THROW ALL OF THE KIDS' CLOTHES
ON THE FLOOR AND PUT JAM ON THE
STAIR RAIL.
AND IT IS NOT MY TITS THAT HAVE
BENT THE GLOBAL ECONOMY TOWARDS
DOMESTIC WORK FOR WOMEN.

Mess is a problem of humanity. Cleaning is the concern of all. A man hiring a male cleaner is simply giving someone a job.

Quite how a straight couple hiring a female cleaner ends up as a crime against feminism isn't clear – unless you believe that running a household is, in some way: a) a womanly duty that can b) only ever be done out of love, and never for cash, because that somehow 'spoils' the magic of the household. As if the dishes know they've been washed by hired help, instead of the woman of the house, and will feel 'all sad'.

This is, clearly – to be exact – total bullshit. Everything else in this world, you can pay someone to do for you. Having a cleaner is nothing to do with feminism.

Feminism has exactly the same problem as 'political correctness' (PCness): people use the phrase without really knowing what it means. A whole generation of people confuse 'feminism' with 'anything to do with women'.

Over the last few years, I've seen feminism – to remind ourselves, the idea that women's pay and power should be equal to that of men – blamed for:

eating disorders
female depression
rising divorce rates
childhood obesity
male depression
women leaving it too late to conceive
the rise in abortion
female binge-drinking
an increase in female crime.

These are all things that have simply INVOLVED WOMEN. They have nothing to do with the rise of 'feminism'.

In the strangest twist of all, feminism is often used as the stick to stop women behaving as freely as men. It is even suggested that acting as freely as men is destroying other women. Like with bitching. There is this idea that feminists aren't meant to bitch about each other. If I slag off another woman, people will say, 'That's not very feminist of you.' Or, 'What about the sisterhood?' Well, I think that feminism will get you so far – and then you have to start bitching. We're feminists – not *Buddhists*.

I have a rule for judging whether some sexist bullshit is happening. It is asking: 'Are the *men* doing it? Are the *men* worrying about this as well? Is this taking up the *men's* time? Are the *men* told not to do this, as it's 'letting the side down'? Are the *men* having to write bloody books about this? Is this making *Jeremy Clarkson* feel insecure?'

Almost always, the answer is: 'No. The boys are not being told they have to be a certain way. They're just... getting on with stuff.'

What is feminism? It is the belief that women should be as free as men, however nuts, dim, deluded, badly dressed, fat, receding, lazy and smug they might be. Are you a feminist? Hahaha. Of course you are.

Chapter 3

I Am Fat!

Now it is 1991, and I am sixteen. I'm sitting on St Peter's lawn with Matthew Vale, smoking. Matt is the coolest teenage boy in Wolverhampton.

It is late October, two months after we first met, and this is the first day out we have had together, alone. I have seen his girlfriend so I know we're not going to 'happen' – unless she suddenly dies, which would be terribly, terribly, TERRIBLY sad.

It's 1991 and I have just got a job. So, for the first time in my life, I can buy clothes from shops, instead of jumble sales. I am wearing a blue tie-dyed shirt over a long skirt, Doc Marten boots and a waistcoat.

I'm sixteen I'm sixteen I'm sixteen and these are my best clothes, and this is my best day. I can wait for him. I'll just wait for him. She might die, after all. She could die so easily. People drop dead on buses all the time.

15

And Matt says: 'Did you have a nickname at school?'

And I say: 'Yes.'

And he says: 'Did they call you Fatty?'

That was the first time I ever felt the world stop. Everything was very cold and still and bright for one second. A flashbulb. Someone has just taken a picture of us, to show again at the end of our lives, in a slide show: 'Here's some of your worst bits!' Me and Matty Vale, on St Peter's lawn, October 1991.

Because I really thought he might not have noticed, hahaha. I thought I'd hidden those extra four stones really carefully, and I was talking too fast for him to see it. I thought my hair was long and shiny and my eyes were blue, and I'd kept it secret. I thought he might not have noticed that I'm fat.

I've said it. Because I am sixteen, sixteen, sixteen and 16 stone. All I do is sit around eating bread and cheese, and reading. I'm fat. But I'm just a brain in a jar, I tell myself. That's my comforting thought. I'm just a brain in a jar. It doesn't matter about the other bits. That is what my body is. 'The other bits.' The jar.

I am clever, so it doesn't matter that I am fat. I am fat. Because I am fully aware of what the word 'fat' really means. It's not just a simple word like 'brunette' or 'thirty-four'. It is a swear word. It is a weapon. It is an attack, brush-off and turn-down. When Matt asks if they used to call me 'Fatty' at school, he is seeing me in the lower orders of the school pecking order. Matt is going to feel sorry for me. Which means he'll never have sex with me. Which means I will die of unhappiness – maybe within the next hour.

When Matty Vale asks me if I used to be called Fatty, I am wearing my swimsuit from when I was twelve under my clothes, and I have been holding my stomach in since midday.

'No!' I say. 'Jesus!'

I take another drag on the fag, and stop holding in my stomach. He's busted me. Why bother. No. They didn't call me Fatty at school, Matt.

It was Fatso.

Is the word 'fat' making you wince when you read it? Does it feel like I'm being rude to say it? It has become a loaded word. It often alarms people and prompts a supportive, scared rush of protest – 'You're not fat! Of course you're not fat! Babe, you're NOT FAT!' – when the person is, clearly and undeniably, fat, and just wants to discuss it.

More often than not it is used as a weapon to stop the talking dead: 'Shut up, you fat bitch.'

Silence. The charge of 'fatness' has replaced 'gay' or 'lesbian' as the playground's favourite abuse. If you can counter a perfectly valid argument with 'Yeah, well, at least I'm not fat', then you have won.

The word is so strong, it still works even if it has no basis in the truth at all. I have seen size-10 women being shut up by this line.

But giving the word 'fat' such power is, of course, no good at all. Just as I have previously urged you to stand on a chair and shout 'I AM A FEMINIST', so I now urge you to stand on a chair and say the word 'FAT'. 'FAT FAT FAT FAT FAT.'

Say it until you lose the bad feeling around it. Say it until it seems normal. Point at things and call them 'fat'. 'That tile is fat.' 'The wall is fat.' 'I believe Jesus is fat.'

The heat needs to be drained out of the word 'fat'. We need to be able to stare, clearly and calmly, right into the middle of fat, and talk about what it is, and what it means, and why it's become the big topic for Western women in the twenty-first century. FAT FAT FAT FAT.

I believe I have got a sensible idea of what a good, 'normal' weight is. What is 'fat' and 'not fat'. And it is: 'Human shaped.' If you look like a human – the kind of shape a ten-year-old would draw – then you are fine. If you can find a dress you look nice in and can run up three flights of stairs, you're not fat. The idea that you need to be better than merely 'human shaped' is basically total bullshit.

My fat years were when I was not human shaped. I was a 16-stone triangle, with triangle legs, and no real neck. And that's because I wasn't doing human things. I didn't walk or run or dance or swim or climb up stairs; the food I ate wasn't the stuff that humans are meant to eat. No one is meant to eat a pound of boiled potatoes covered in Vitalite, or a fist-sized lump of cheese. I had no connection to my body. I didn't understand my body. I was just a brain in a jar. I wasn't a woman.

After he smashed my heart to bits, it was actually Matthew Vale who knocked four stone off me. On Thursday and Friday nights, we start climbing over the railings of the dual carriageway to a pub in the middle of nowhere. We spend hours dancing to records. He also gets me onto ten Silk Cut a day, which leaves me no money for lunch – useful.

Speeded-up CCTV film would show me turning from something Flump-like into something that is a human-shaped teenage girl. I can now go out and buy a dress, from a normal shop.

A short flowery one, to be worn with cardi, boots and eyeliner. I can pass for 'normal', if I dress carefully.

I still never use the words 'thin' or 'fat', in case anyone starts looking more closely. More importantly, on that tiny dance floor I feel a new-found joy: I've found out where my body is. Turns out, it was RIGHT UNDER MY HEAD, ALL ALONG! WHO KNEW? It's always the last place you look.

And now I can make it spin over here, badly. And leap over there, insanely. And pretend to play invisible maracas in a dance move that surely keeps me a virgin for another year, minimum. But it's fun, having these arms, and these legs, and this little belly. And it's the start of a slow process of getting to the point where, at forty-five, I can say I like my body as much as my head. We're all friends now. We get on, and we agree on things, such as what a 'reasonable' amount of crisps adds up to, and whether I should run up the escalator (yes).

Chapter 4

I Encounter Some Sexism!

So, I have lost weight, I can wear a dress, and I have got a job. I am now the Least Important Person at *Melody Maker*, the weekly music paper that everyone confuses with *NME*.

Going into the adult world is a shock. I have already decided I'm going to have sex with as many people as I can. There is no reason not to crack on with my plan.

Flirting in the workplace is a tricky subject for feminists. Many hardcore feminists don't believe in it at all. As far as they're concerned, you might as well go for it and just install yourself in a window in Soho. And you know, for many, that's the right view to take. Some women just don't flirt. It makes them tetchy, and they don't like it, and they'd rather not bother. But for other women, flirting's just ... how it comes out.

As a cheerful, born flirt, my thinking is, if you're going to spend all day talking to people why not try to make it end with everyone feeling a bit perky?

Did flirting help me at *Melody Maker*? Did I further my career on the basis of my sexual allure? I must be brisk here: no. Almost all my bosses seemed to regard me as some kind of chimp in a dress who'd climbed in through an open window.

So, no. I did not further my career by flirting. However, I truly believe that, should they wish to, serious feminists are allowed to flirt their way to the top. After all, *men* are basically flirting with each other all the time. Bonding over football, and going to the pub – the average workplace is basically romance for all genders. So I am learning about flirting. Not for business – just for fun.

God it's tricky. I've only ever flirted with teenage boys before, who don't really notice it half the time, God bless them. So the next time a man comes up to me, we talk about Erasure for five minutes, then he suggests I move over slightly, so he can get served, and then I stare at the man, silently.

'You OK?' he asks, finally, looking a little worried, holding out a fiver to the barman for his beer.

'I was just wondering what it would be like to kiss you,' I reply, giving him an intense stare from beneath the hat.

At the time, I'm not aware of it, but looking back now I suspect I looked like a cross-eyed clam, looking for careless plankton. Ten seconds later, and we're kissing. I am so happy. My God! Who knew it was this easy! That you can just ask for some sexual contact – and get it!

The next few weeks are amazing. I pretty much put my career on hold to go round getting kissed as much as possible. But the music and media industry is a tiny world and I start to get a 'bad name' back at *Melody Maker*.

On the one hand, I can see why I have become a running gag in the office. I am acting like a sexed-up lady Pac-Man – running around flapping my mouth open and closed, gobbling up people's faces. It's certainly worth a good hundred gags or so. Hell, I'm making about fifty on the topic myself.

But the jokes are not 'amused' jokes. There is an odd air to the comments; there's a kind of … poking, pinching, mean tone to them. And I notice that these jokes aren't being made about the men in the office who are kissing me. It feels like these jokes are coming from a dark place.

*

Then, one day, one of the editors calls me over to his desk, and tells me the feature I've just written *could* be a cover story, 'So why don't you sit on my lap, while we talk about it?'

Wow, I think. This is some sexism! Some sexism is happening to me! In some respects, it's almost exciting. After all, the last time I was being judged about my sexuality, was when The Yobs were throwing gravel at me on my birthday. If I've gone from being wholly horrible (then) to being looked down on as a slag (now), this is, surely … *a bit of a progress?* I've gone up in the world! However, I still don't know how to deal with it.

In the end, I simply regress back into the coping methods of my childhood. As the editor pats his lap – waiting for me to sit on it – I simply think, 'More fool you, dude,' and *slam* myself down on his knees, heavily, and light a fag.

'Lost feeling in your legs yet?' I ask, cheerfully, as he sweats and coughs.

I get the front cover. He spends ten minutes in the meeting room, banging his thighs until he gets the blood back in his legs, as his mates laugh at him. I have beaten this sly sexism.

It never used to be like this. In the old days, sexism was more obvious. You knew sexism when you met it. It was all, 'Know your limits, women,' 'Make us a cup of tea, love,' 'Look at the rack on THAT,' and wolf whistles from any passing male over the age of twelve.

Of course, there is still plenty of this old-fashioned sexism around today. I asked on Twitter if anyone had had any sexism recently. I wasn't expecting the flood that started thirty seconds after I asked. In the end, I had nearly 2,000 replies.

When I asked the ladies of Twitter for their examples of sexism some replies were disturbing. Kate explained that she 'no longer wears a white top and black skirt to meetings, since a queue formed in front of me at a coffee break. They all thought I was a waitress'.

Or Hannah, who – on being made jobless – was comforted by her boss with the comment, 'Don't worry, love – at least you still have great legs.'

Of course, the reason these examples are so harmful is the doubt involved. Are they being sexist on purpose, or is it just an accident? Are you going to look like you have no sense of humour if you call people out on this? Should you just let it pass when some man who is your junior at work sees you standing next to a tea urn, and asks you for 'Milk, no sugar – and you got any Hobnobs?'

In short, how can you tell when some sexism is happening to you? Simply ask: Is this polite? If we – the population of the earth, male and female alike – are just 'The Guys', then was one of The Guys just ... rude to a fellow Guy? Don't call it sexism. Call it 'manners', instead.

When a woman blinks a little, then says, 'I'm sorry, but that sounded a little ... uncivil,' a man is likely to say sorry. Because even the most rampant bully on earth has no defence against a charge of simply being rude. After all, you can argue – argue until you cry – about what modern contempt for women is. But straight-up rudeness, of the kind his mother would clatter the back of his head for, is clear. It doesn't need to be a 'man vs woman' thing. It's just a tiff between The Guys.

Seeing the whole world as 'The Guys' is important. The idea that we're all just a bunch of well-meaning guys, trying to get along, is the basics of my world view. I'm neither 'pro-women' nor 'anti-men'. I'm just 'Thumbs up for the seven billion people in the world.' Because I don't think that 'men'/maleness/male sexuality is the problem here. I don't think sexism is a 'man vs woman' thing. What I see, instead, is winner vs loser.

Most sexism is down to men being used to us being the losers. That's what the problem is. We just have bad status. Come on – let's admit it. Let's stop pretending that there is an equal history of women winning and being creative. There isn't. Until recently, *we just weren't allowed to.*

The history of men's work, wars and art started 40,000 years ago. But women – we weren't even allowed to *have* most jobs until the twentieth century. We were legally *owned* by our husbands. The history of men is thousands of years old. But the history of women has only just started. Women – we are a *new thing*. And that's exciting.

Chapter 5

I Am In Love!

A year later, and I am in love. He's The One. Obviously, I thought the one before him was The One, and the one before that was The One, too. Frankly, I'm so into the idea of being in love that anyone could be The One. But, no – this, now, is definitely The One. The very One.

We are walking down grey pavements in Hampstead in March, hand in hand, and I am so in love. It must be said that I feel terrible, and he's a total arsehole, but I am in love. Finally. By sheer force of will. I've got a person, all of my own.

'You walk funny,' he says, in an oddly rude way. 'You don't walk like a fat girl.'

I have no idea what he means. I let go of his hand.

I'm in love. Christ, it's miserable.

So yes, he's a boy in a band – the first boy in a band I could get. Insanely talented, very beautiful, but also very lazy, and really troubled. His band gets nowhere because he refuses to do 'shitty gigs' he thinks are beneath him.

Even though we are going out with each other, and he's moved into my flat, I don't think he likes me. When I write, he sits next to me on a chair, and explains at great length how he's more talented than me. When we're with friends, he'll make a joke and – when I laugh – snap, 'Why are you laughing? You don't understand what I'm talking about.'

My family hate him. Caz is brisk about him: 'He is a cock. You were better off when you were just living with the mice in your kitchen. He's a short man with a girl's name – and that's trouble.'

His name is Courtney. And he is quite short, and very thin: he's clearly smaller than me. I feel like I'm too big for him. This is a problem. I feel like, if I stood up straight, I'd crush him.

Over at Pete from *Melody Maker*'s house, I get tearful and sit under the table all night, crying. Most of all – despite waiting my whole life to leave home – I'm missing my family. At night, when I lie in bed with Courtney, I find myself thinking of my double bed back in Wolverhampton, with my sister Prinnie in it. I may often have woken up soaked in her urine, but I always felt safe there, I think, as I lie in the dark. I wish Prinnie was in the bed, instead of Courtney.

I am talking about Courtney to everyone. I am a bore. It feels like our being together is a huge puzzle that, if I apply myself to it enough, I will solve, and gain the result of True Love. After all, all the pieces needed for us to be the perfect couple are there. He's a man, I'm a woman, and we live in the same house. All the other stuff – getting on, courtesy, tenderness, not wanting to kill each other – are little things I can work on, if I think about them enough.

Caz endures my attempts to work out the answer. It's amazing how much you can find to say when there's one big thing you're too afraid to say: 'This isn't working.'

The problem is that I am the problem. Courtney is just unhappy. I know that. I know it in my bones. When I find the way to make him happy, everything will be fine. He's broken, and I must fix him – and then the good bit of our being together will start to happen. This is just the tricky, early bit of love, where I undo all the bad stuff, and let him finally be who he is, secretly, inside. Secretly, inside, he does love me. My strength will prove it. If it doesn't work, it's simply because I didn't try hard enough.

This is all proven when I find his diary, while he's out. I know I shouldn't read it – but, in a way, I'm reading it for us. If it is a sin, then it's one of those good sins you hear so much about. A love sin. Because if I find out what he's really thinking, then our being together will finally blossom.

The diary is pretty clear. 'She's mad,' he writes, of me. 'When is she going to start taking me to celebrity parties? I'm stuck at home, bored. When is this going to be good for my career?'

Further entries reveal he's still in love with a girl from his hometown, who sacked him off three years ago. Seeing this as Courtney merely feeling 'insecure' in our relationship, I try harder. I cook for him, to make our house seem like a home. I stroke his head when he complains about how little success his band are having. And I crush the music-writer thoughts in my head, like: Well, if you actually played a couple of fucking gigs, you might get somewhere.

I escape the house with our stupid new dog – now old – and walk to the Heath. I lie under a tree – dressed in my nightie, with a coat thrown over it – and stare up at the leaves. I skin up a joint – just a small one. The people around you are mirrors, I think to myself. You see yourself reflected in their eyes. If the mirror is true, and smooth, you see your true self. That's how you learn who you are.

When I look in Courtney's eyes, I see a crazy, bossy woman who is trying to ruin him. I pause. I love him, but he hates me. That's what I see. I will have to tell Courtney to leave. I can't live with him any more.

I go home.

Courtney won't leave.

'I'm not going until I can find a flat as nice as this,' he says, firmly. 'I'm not going to go and live somewhere shitty. I'm not going to break up with you and live in fucking ... Cricklewood. That wouldn't be fair.' He announces that night we won't fuck any more: 'I'm too depressed to fuck you,' he says. 'Fucking you will make things worse.'

The mirror gets darker. I almost can't see my face.

A weekend away! That's what we need. Fresh air and the countryside. We just need to get out of London. It's London that's the problem: London, with Cricklewood in it, which Courtney fears. We'll be fine somewhere else. Some friends of Courtney's are recording their new album in Wales, and invite a group of us to go and stay with them for the weekend.

As far as everyone thinks, Courtney and I are still the hot couple on the block: the pop star and the teenage TV presenter, partying all night long. Only Caz knows the truth, from all those 2 a.m. phone calls. She sits opposite me now, on the train out of Paddington, heading west. I invited her at the last minute – promising her the chance to hang out with a famous band, and drink as much as she likes.

'I wouldn't come if it was a band I liked,' she says, when I ask her. 'That would be weird. But given that I think they're a bunch of tossers, I'll come. Drinking huge amounts of famous arseholes' champagne is the duty of the true rebel.'

We've all ordered drinks from the onboard bar – the train is the pre-show party. I'm reading *Private Eye*, and laughing.

On my third laugh, Courtney snaps, 'Stop laughing. You've made your point.'

'I'm just ... laughing,' I say.

'No – that's not your normal laugh,' Courtney says. He's drunker than everyone else. 'You only laugh like that around other people.'

Everyone has gone silent. This is awkward.

'I think she's just ... laughing, Courtney,' Caz says, sharply. 'Although I can see why that might not be something you've heard a great deal, and that it might alarm you.'

I kick Caz under the table to shut up. I feel embarrassed that she is now having to deal with our secret blackness. This is private. The inside of my soul. I should be able to contain it. I just won't laugh any more.

At Rockfield, autumn is painfully beautiful: a Welsh autumn makes an English summer look childish, and flat. The frost spangles the side of the mountain. Caz and I stand in the driveway, cramming blackberries into our mouths, and then chase each other around a field, like kids. The air is hard, like iron. I laugh madly, and then find myself worrying.

'Has my laugh changed?' I ask Caz. 'Does it sound more ... London-y?'

'That is, without doubt, the stupidest question I have ever been asked,' Caz says.

The studio is where Queen recorded 'Bohemian Rhapsody'. Courtney is thrilled to be in a proper studio: 'Finally, I'm home!' he says, slouching in a swivel chair, and strumming on one of the band's very expensive Martin guitars. He starts to play a couple of their hits – but with new lyrics 'that I've written myself'. The band listen, politely, but they clearly wish he'd stop.

'Woo! It's a live happening! I can review it!' I say, trying to move the mood on.

'Not unless you've learned how to write yet,' Courtney replies, strumming a G minor, and puffing on a fag.

I'm so embarrassed that I take Ecstasy, just for something to do with my face. As the E warms up inside, and the rest of the room melts, I see Caz is quietly watching me.

Before today, I haven't seen her for months – so long I'd almost forgotten who I am when I'm with her. Her face becomes a mirror: I can see reflected in it a teenage girl with blasted pupils, sitting alone on a chair, looking very, very tired, even though I am talking fast.

She is a true mirror, I think. I should look into her more often. I can see myself in there. I can see my good points and my bad points – but I know that face. I feel like I haven't seen that face in a long, long time. Not since I was a child. We stare at each other for an age – just good, old-fashioned off-your-face staring.

In the end, Caz just raises an eyebrow at me. I know what she's saying. She's saying: 'What?'

I mouth back: 'I hate him.'

She mouths back: 'That's because he's a knob-skin. They're all knob-skins.'

I go and sit next to Caz, on the floor. Caz and I have maracas. We are shaking them in a way that can only be called 'sarcastic beat'. Every so often, someone asks us to stop – but we just start again, very quietly, a minute later. It's making us happy.

I don't know how long we've been sitting like this when Courtney comes over and looks down at us. 'Hello ladies,' he says. He's grinding his teeth quite badly.

We shake our maracas at him. My pupils are blasted. Caz's are like saucers.

'Hello, Courtney,' Caz says. She manages to put a vast amount of hatred in every letter of his name, while still sounding civil.

'We were all wondering – could you stop the maracas now?' Courtney says, with over-the-top politeness.

'I'm afraid we can't,' Caz replies, with equal politeness.

'Why?' Courtney asks. He speaks with icy courtesy.

There is a pause.

'Because you're a total dick,' Caz says, as if she is the Queen. She shakes her maraca, to stress what she has just said.

Before I can stop myself, I laugh – a gigantic, unsexy honk, with a definite Wolverhampton accent. 'He is!' I say, joyfully. I am thrilled to have seen the truth. 'A total dick!'

We shake our maracas in unison.

'Courtney, I'm going to go home and change the locks,' I say, cheerfully.

Still holding hands, me and Caz stand. 'We're going to order a cab now,' I say, to the room. 'Thank you for having us, everybody.'

Courtney's shouting something, but I can't really hear him. We leave the room at high speed, running as fast as we can now, to get a cab; to get back to London; to find some chewing gum, to stop this constant teeth-grinding.

We've just ordered a cab from Reception when I realise I have left one important thing undone.

'Stay there,' I say to Caz.

'Where are you going?' she yells.

'STAY THERE!' I bellow, running back down the corridor.

I burst into the studio. Everyone looks up. Courtney looks at me with a mix of fury, self-pity, and a vast amount of cocaine. But he looks like he will take me back, if I truly say sorry. If I really mean it. If I love him. If, in my heart, I love him.

'Can we keep the maracas?' I ask.

Chapter 6

I Get Married!

So what has my sister Caz been up to, in all this time?

Many things.

She's cut her hair short, written three plays, racked up an awesome collection of drum'n'bass records. She's been part of the creative bar-keeping team that came up – one desperate Christmas – with the Sherry Cappuccino: a brave, but doomed, concept. Sherry curdles in milk. We now know that as a fact.

But what she's mainly been doing is going to a lot of weddings.

This is unfortunate, because Caz hates weddings.

'Five weddings in four years,' she wailed after the last, and most disastrous, one, taking her muddy shoes off, and throwing them in the sink. The wedding had been held in a field. In the rain. Some cows chased the guests during the reception. 'I really hope no one else I know ever, ever falls in love again. People finding true love works out badly for me.'

Of course, people finding true love works out badly for everyone, really. I mean, it's OK in the end – once everyone settles down, and stops making a big fuss about it. But fairly near the beginning, there is a massive test of everyone's patience and love – a wedding.

Weddings are our fault, ladies. Every aspect of their awfulness happened because of us. And you know what? Not only have we let humanity down, we've let ourselves down, too.

Weddings do women no good at all. Whenever I think about weddings, I want to run into the church – like Dustin Hoffman in *The Graduate* – and shout 'STOP! STOP THE WEDDINGS!' And when the organ has ground to a halt, and everyone turns around to stare at me, and the vicar has stopped stuttering, 'Well, really!' in a stern manner, I'm going to rock up to the pulpit – tearing my stupid bloody hat off as I go – light a fag, lean back, and this is the sermon I will preach.

1) COST.
Ladies! Being a woman is already very, very expensive. Tampons, hairdressers, child-care,

beauty aids, women's shoes being three times more costly than men's. The cost of the things we need (Lil-Lets) plus the things we feel naked without (proper haircut) is already ruinous. And that's before we factor in women earning 30 per cent less than men. And women being the ones who usually have to watch their career go all Titanic when the question of 'Who will look after the kids?' raises its head.

In the old days, a dowry would often be one of the deciding factors of a woman's life: how much money her parents could give to a marriage, fixing whom a woman could and couldn't marry.

These days, of course, a woman is free to marry whoever she chooses. And yet, marriage still often involves crippling sums of money – the average cost of a UK wedding is £30,000. This is now commonly paid for by the couple themselves, in some kind of bizarre, in-the-end-useless but self-imposed dowry.

Spending £30,000 at a stage in your life when you are – usually – still pretty poor and trying to buy things like 'a house' and 'things to eat', seems pretty baffling, whichever way you slice it. And not least when one in four marriages ends in divorce. Personally, I wouldn't spend £30,000 on anything that either a) didn't have doors and windows, or b) couldn't grant me three wishes. £30,000 is an absurd amount of money to spend on something. It is insanity.

What the £30,000 buys you is Aspect Two of why weddings are so bad for women:

2) THE BEST DAY OF YOUR LIFE.
'It's the best day of your life.' Well. The snags here are obvious.

Of course it's not the best day of your life. A day that was really the best day of your life wouldn't involve: Uncle Wrong, Aunt Drip, and someone from your office you had to invite, because, if you don't, you will spend the next six years being sulked at every time you pass them in a stairwell. Clearly, your wedding is actually like some unholy mix of a works away-day and family therapy. It should, therefore, be tackled with the same mixture of quiet resolve and heavy drinking.

Also, bear this in mind, ladies – the phrasing: 'the best day of your life'. Yes, the best day of your life: the bride. Not anyone else's. Let's face it, the groom has quietly not given a shit about the event, from beginning to end. Weddings are basically something that brides invite grooms along to as an after-thought – and a thought that came after working out which trios of

41

chocolate puddings were going to be served, at that.

Women start planning their weddings when they're five, for goodness' sake. When they have no idea who they'll marry, and just imagine an Action Man's body with a blur where his face is instead. So it's clearly not the best day of the groom's life. And it's also not the best day of any of the guests' lives, either. Because weddings aren't fun for the guests. It's something we're wholly aware of when we're guests – 300 miles from home, in a pashmina, making awkward chitty-chat with a bleary drunkard on the table clearly called 'The Dregs' in the placement plans.

We forget this the minute we start planning our own weddings. I did it myself.

Up until my actual wedding, I'd done everything brilliantly. I had so not been a twat about being in love. I wasn't over-dramatic or attention-seeking. I had got over breaking up with Courtney by making a cheerful badge that read 'I Went Out With Satan – And Survived!' and wearing it to all social events. I didn't mope and I didn't sulk – instead, I made up for a year of fruitless fidelity by cheerfully going back out into the world and seeing if there was any fun left out there for me.

As it turned out, there was loads. I was happy to note that getting back out 'on the dating scene' needed absolutely no effort or worry at all. For a month, I rode some kind of relaxed sex galleon around London, like a lady pirate. I was recalling, again, how every chat with a member of the opposite sex carries with it that tiny, atom-small, atomic-bright chance: 'Hello. Are you "it"?'

And every Thursday, I would invite over Pete from *Melody Maker*, cook him soup, and tell him all these stories – 'So I rang down to Room Service, and asked for a steak sandwich, and a pair of men's pants' – while we played records, and cried laughing.

Then, in the middle of February, my mood, suddenly, changed. I woke one Monday morning to find an odd, heavy unhappiness had taken over. It wasn't depression, or misery – it was both more restless, and more hopeful, than that. I felt in limbo: a mix of waiting for something, and missing something terribly – even though I'd never had it. Indeed, not only had I never had it – I also had no idea what it was.

The source of my blues absolutely baffled me. I spent a week wandering around my flat, deflated – clueless as to what it meant. I'd pick something up – my phone, a record, a fag – and then put them down again, sadly, going, 'No, that's not it.'

Twice I went to the shops to buy food and, half-way around the supermarket, I'd think, 'When I get back, it might have happened!' I'd bustle back, full of energy and hope again, and burst into the flat – only to find it exactly as I'd left it.

Whatever it was still hadn't arrived. The let-down was crushing.

After a week of this, on the Sunday night, my sub-conscious – as if driven mad by my dimness – finally spelt it out for me. I went to bed drunk, and dreamed I was on the escalators at Baker Street underground station, going up. The escalators seemed impossibly high. I couldn't even see the top. It was going to be a long, long time before I got to the exit.

'It's going to take for ever to get up there!' I called out.

'It's OK,' a voice said. I turned around, and saw Pete, standing behind me. 'I'm here,' he said, simply.

'Oh!' I said, waking up. 'Oh! I'm in love! I'm in love with Pete.' I looked around the flat. 'He's what's not here.'

Six years and a £19.99 engagement ring later, and it's our wedding day. It was – at first – going to be in a registry office, in London, followed by a reception at a pub. In boring, empty mid-October. Everyone could have got the bus home. It would have cost less than 200 quid. We could have knocked it all off in five hours flat.

Oh, I wish we'd had that wedding.

After I'd inhaled 600 bridal magazines and taken into account a few requests from the in-laws, however, it ended up being in a former monastery in Coventry, two days after Christmas.

It was also Caz's birthday. She has always borne the brunt of the love of others.

I don't want to overstate it but, by God, it was a bad wedding. Here I am, at twenty-four, waiting to come down the aisle in my red velvet dress, with ivy in my hair. My lifelong curse of not being able to find shoes I can walk in extends even to here, on my most glamorous day – under the satin-edged velvet, I'm wearing a manky pair of Doc Marten sandals.

My father is in a shop-lifted suit and shoes – but he looks calm, wise and even a bit emotional about giving away his first child in marriage. 'Oh, my lovely daughter,' he says, smelling a little of whisky. 'My kitten-cat.' His eyes have the faint shine of tears in them.

As the music strikes up in the next room, he takes my arm, and leans in to whisper something. This is where he tells me something of how he and Mum have stayed together for twenty-four years, and had eight kids, I think to myself. This is going to be one of our great bonding moments. Oh Lord, I hope he doesn't make me cry. I have so much eyeliner on.

'Darling girl,' he says, as the usher opens the door, and I see the whole crowd crane around, to watch my entrance. 'Darling love. Remember you're a Womble.'

An hour later, and everyone's in the bar. My family are enjoying the free bar – many of them can't walk any more, and, of the ones that can, two of them have found a memorial to a dead knight, and are giving his statue a 'saucy' pole dance. My dad, meanwhile, has managed to spill candle wax all over his shirt and has – on the advice of others – taken it off, and put it into a freezer in the kitchen, to harden the wax. He is now sitting at the table in his vest and jacket, drinking Guinness, looking bleary.

By the time the reception starts, a quiet air of failure fills the event. By 10 p.m., most people have gone to bed early – trying to save something from being dragged to an expensive hotel in the middle of their holidays. I like to think they are all eating sausage rolls, stolen from the buffet, and watching *Cheers*. I am happy for them. I wish I were one of them.

At 10.23 p.m., the fire alarm goes off. As everyone goes out onto the lawn and shivers, I notice all my siblings are missing. Going back into the hotel to find them, I knock on the door of my sister's room. I find all seven siblings in here – standing on the bed, waving room-service menus under the smoke detector.

'Why aren't you leaving?' I ask, standing in the doorway in my wedding dress. They turn to face me. They are all wearing balloon crowns made by the Balloon Animal man we'd hired to entertain the kids. Eddie is holding a balloon sword.

'It's sensed our body heat!' Weena says, stoned, and panicked. 'There's only supposed to be two people in here, but we all bunked in, and now it's overheated the room! We're trying to cool it down!'

They carry on waving their room-service menus at the ceiling. The fire alarm stops ringing. It's 10.32 p.m. I'm married. I go to bed. In the following twenty-one years, not one guest ever mentions our wedding again. We all seem to silently agree that it's for the best.

Chapter 7

I Get Into Fashion!

At the age of twenty-four, I look in my wardrobe and think, 'I'm not a proper woman.' All the other women are 'putting together outfits' and 'working their looks'. I am just 'putting together the cleanest things'. Having been an indie-kid, I come from a scene where you boast about how little you spent on an outfit – 'I found this jacket in a *skip!* On a *dead man!* Under a *fox carcass!'* We don't 'do' fashion. But I'm starting to feel too old for this. I feel like I should, finally, sort this out, and wear clothes I haven't found in an actual bin. So I start 'engaging with fashion'.

Man, but it's harder than it looks! You find 'the dress' – but then 'the dress' must have 'the belt', and then a bag that goes with it, and some clashing tights that give it a 'pop' – and so on, and so on, like an endless quest. It's all bloody knackering, to be honest. But I am a noble and brave woman! *I* will master this!

So here is what, twenty-one years later, I have learned about fashion.

Shoes

I've spent my whole life in trainers, or boots, but it's clear that, if I am to properly be a woman, I will just have to go out and get some heels. The women's magazines I read are all clear about heels: they are part of being a woman.

'No one messes with a woman in heels,' one feature in *Elle* decides. 'They are your greatest weapons in the style wars.'

This shit sounds serious.

The next day, I go out and buy my first pair of high heels. They make my feet sweat and they're also quite painful in both the toe and heel area – but no matter! I am in heels! I am a woman!

That night, I wear them to a gig, and fall down a staircase in them. Amazingly, I don't see this for what it is – an obvious clue that I can't wear heels. I just think, 'I don't have the *right* heels yet! Gotta buy some more!'

Two decades on, and I now have a great many more pairs of high heels. And a great many more stories about how wearing them has ended badly for me. In fact, I have a whole box full of such shoes under my bed. Each pair was bought in hope of a new life I had seen in a magazine, and thought I would find, now I had the 'right' shoes.

Each pair has stayed unworn since the first day I wore them, and fell over/twisted my ankle/spent all night sitting on a chair, as I just could not stand up in them without shouting 'WHY MUST THESE HURT SO MUCH!'

But I know that I am not alone. *All* women have one of these piles of Unworn Shoes hidden in the house. Why are all these shoes unworn?

Ladies, I'm going to put it on the line. I'm going to say what, over the past twenty-one years, I have realised. Something that we all secretly knew anyway, the first time we put heels on: that there's only ten people in the world, tops, who should actually wear heels. And six of those are drag queens. The rest of us just need to … give up. Surrender. Finally give in to what nature is telling us. We can't walk in them. WE CANNOT WALK IN THE DAMN THINGS.

The absolute fact that high heels cannot be worn is self-evident all around us – coming to a head at the average wedding, where every woman is wearing heels. In our minds, we are serene and elegant women in our finest. In truth, of course, we're staggering around in agony.

By the time the dancing kicks in, 80 per cent of the women are barefoot or in tights – the edge of the room full of ditched kitten-heels and stilettoes. Women spend more time shopping for shoes *for* a wedding than they spend time actually wearing them *at* a wedding. At the end of the evening, all these women have to get men to carry them to their cabs, so their tights don't 'get dirty' on the way out to the cab.

But, oddly, we still totally accept the uselessness of heels. We don't care about the thousands of pounds, over a lifetime, we spend on shoes we only wear once, and in great pain. Indeed, we're oddly proud of it.

So why do we believe that wearing heels is an important part of being a woman, despite knowing it doesn't work? Why do we obsess over these things that make us walk like mad ducks? Was Germaine Greer right? Is the heel just to catch the eyes of men, and get laid?

The answer is, of course, no. Women wear heels because they think they make their legs look thinner. END OF. They think that by basically walking on tiptoes, they're slimming their legs down from a size 14 to a size 10. But they aren't, of course. There is only one precedent for 'a fat leg shrinking down to a point' – and it's on a pig.

So, at forty-five, I've jacked it in. I have, finally, given up on heels.

Indeed, I've pretty much given up on women's shoes altogether. Even women's flats seem flimsy compared to men's. I've got men's riding boots, men's biker boots, men's brogues, some Doc Martens. They are all beautifully made, comfortable, and cheaper than the ones in the women's section.

I've decided I'm now on strike when it comes to women's shoes. I'm going to sit out the entire world of chick footwear until designers make some that it's possible to walk in, for more than an hour. And to walk with the easy stride of Gene Kelly about to break into a routine, and no day-long pain afterwards.

If I'm going to spunk £500 on a pair of designer shoes, it's going to be a pair that a) I can dance to 'Bad Romance' in, and b) will allow me to run away from a murderer, should one suddenly decide to give chase. That's the minimum I ask from my footwear. To be able to dance in it, and for it not to get me murdered.

Handbags

The other fashion item women are supposed to go mad for is the handbag. Apart from shoes, a handbag is the only other item you're never too fat to fit into.

By the time I was thirty-five, I'd had two children, paid off half my mortgage, got drunk with Lady Gaga, and could make all my own dips. I could do thirty seconds of the easy bit of the 'Single Ladies' dance, had two opposite opinions about global trade, knew how to stop someone choking, and once scored 420 in Scrabble. But I didn't yet have an 'investment handbag'.

My stance on 'investment handbags' has always been that if I were going to make a £600 investment, it would probably be in Post Office bonds – and not in something that lives on the floor in pubs, or which I sometimes use to carry 5lb of potatoes home.

But I am aware that I am in a handbag minority. Normal women, says *Grazia*, do not buy one handbag every five years for £45 from Topshop, like I do. Normal women have dozens of handbags: small ones, potato-less ones, £600 investment ones such as a Mulberry tote.

With growing worry, I learned that having a £600 handbag is like having a crush on the Joker in Batman. You MUST do it. It is a vital part of being a woman.

I made a decision. One of the modern wisdoms of womanhood is that eBay has fake designer handbags that you can't tell from the real thing. But despite typing 'great fake £600 handbags for £100' into the 'Search' field, nothing came up.

On page 14 of my search results I finally saw one I liked, by Marc Jacobs. It was bright, acid-house yellow, with a picture of Debbie Harry on it. But my joy in finding a £600 bag I liked was dimmed when it turned out to be a canvas tote, for £17. Basically, the only designer item I was attracted to, was a Marc Jacobs carrier bag.

Anyway, let's face it: the actual handbag is neither here nor there – it's what you keep in it that's the most important thing. I have – after years of study on the subject – come up with the definitive list of what you ACTUALLY need in your handbag:

1) Something that can absorb huge amounts of liquid
2) Eyeliner
3) Safety pin
4) Biscuit

This covers everything. You will need nothing else.

Clothes

So that's my feet, and what I'm keeping my fags in. But what am I wearing, now? As a strident feminist, how am I dressed?

Here is what I have learned about clothes:

1) Leopardskin is a neutral.
2) You can get away with nearly anything if you wear the thing with black opaque tights and boots.
3) Most people are wrong about belts. A belt is often not a good friend to a lady. Indeed, it often acts merely as a visual aid to help the onlooker settle the question: 'Which half is fatter – the bottom or the top?'
4) Bright red is a neutral.
5) Sellotape is NOT strong enough to mend a hole in the crotch of a pair of tights.
6) You should NOT buy an outfit if you have to strike a sexy pose in the changing-room mirror to make it look good. On the other hand, if you start dancing the minute you put it on, buy it, however much it costs. Unless it's lots, in which case, you can't, so don't.
7) You are very, very unlikely to look bad in an above-the-knee, fitted, 1950s-style dress with sleeves, and a cardigan.

8) The most flattering trousers you'll ever have are some black running trousers with a fiercely high Lycra content. They make your thighs and arse look tiny. You spend over two years trying to pluck up the courage to wear them out with a pair of knee-high boots and a jacket, but always bottle it at the last minute. It is a source of lasting regret.

9) Silver lamé is a neutral.

10) Ditto gold sequin.

11) Instead of buying something that says 'Dry clean only', just put £50 in the garment's pocket, and walk out of the shop, leaving garment and money on the hanger. In the long run it will save you money, time, and the need to squirt Sure Extra onto the armpits.

12) Everything from Per Una at Marks & Spencer makes you look a little bit mental. I don't know why this should be so, but it is true.

And this is everything I have learned about fashion.

Chapter 8

Why You Should Have Children

A Bad Birth

It was no surprise to me to discover I was terrible at giving birth. No surprise at all.

All that I know about birth is what I've seen from my mother – returning after delivering each one of my siblings as white as death. She hobbled into the house seven times with a bad story: a breech, an emergency Caesarean, a trapped nerve, a tangled cord.

So when I become pregnant at twenty-four, I don't think I can do it. I don't know how you do it. I'm insanely, wilfully ignorant. At my six-month check-up, I comment on an odd, modern sculpture above the bed. In white plastic, it seems to show ten pupil-less eyes getting gradually wider, as if in alarm.

'What's that?' I ask, cheerfully.

'It's the stages of cervical dilation,' the midwife says, puzzled. 'From nought to ten centimetres.'

'The ... cervix?' I say. 'Why does the cervix dilate?'

'That's how the baby comes out,' the midwife says, now looking like she's talking to a madwoman. 'That's what labour is – the cervix gradually dilating, to let the baby out.'

'The cervix?' I repeat, wholly alarmed. 'A baby can't come out of that! It's not a hole! I've felt it! That's a solid thing!'

'Well, that's why it's all a ... bit of an effort,' the midwife replies, as gently as she can.

At that point, I know I can't have a baby. I can't open my cervix. I wouldn't even know where to start.

When my contractions finally start, they are painful, yet useless. The baby is in the posterior position – her skull grinds against my spine. The midwives sadly explain that posterior labours are long and hard.

After twenty-four sleepless hours, they suggest hospital. I cry. They insist.

And in the brightness of the ward, a sour-faced Swedish midwife assesses me as I sit on the bed, weeping.

From Saturday night until Monday morning, the NHS slowly and dutifully goes through its list of actions to bail out failed women.

My waters are unbroken – they break them with a crochet hook.

My contractions have stopped – they jump-start them.

My cervix is firm – painfully, they sweep it, just as a contraction starts. It feels a little like being diced, internally, at the start of slow murder.

Of course, after two days of this, the baby started to die.

On the monitor, her heartbeat sounds like a tiny toy drum. As each contraction squeezes her, you can hear the drum getting fainter. I was meat and pain, pinned in place by monitor wires, and my mother had never taught me how to turn inside out.

In the end, I'd been going for three days and nights. The doctors had to strap me down and cut me open.

For the next year, every Monday at 7.48 a.m., I would look at the clock and remember the birth. I would tremble and give thanks it was all over, and marvel that we both survived. Lizzie was born at 8.32 a.m. – but 7.48 a.m. was when they gave me the drugs, and the pain, finally, stopped.

Pain changes you. We are programmed for it to be the fastest lesson we'll ever learn. I learned two things from the first baby I had:

1) That being very unfit, attending only two NCT birth classes, and genuinely believing that I would probably die was not a good way to prepare for labour, all things told.
2) That once you have felt such pain, the rest of your life becomes relatively easy.

However awful an experience, it's really not wasted. Because you know what you get? Perspective – a new angle on life. A whole heap of perspective.

I do not mean this in a wanky way. But in many cases, a furious, twenty-four-hour dose of wildly intolerable pain sorts out many of the more fretful, gloomy aspects of modern life. It is like a mental bushfire. You get rid of a lot of emotional dead wood. To be frank, childbirth gives a woman a huge set of balls. The 'high' you get, as you realise it's all over and that you didn't actually die, can last the rest of your life.

Off their faces, and bucked by how brave they were, new mothers finally tell the in-laws to back off. They dye their hair red, get driving lessons, go self-employed, learn to use a drill, and try Thai condiments. They make cheerful jokes about weeing by mistake, and stop being scared of the dark. In short, a dose of pain that intense turns you from a girl into a woman. There are other ways of gaining the same effect but, minute for minute, it's one of the best ways of changing your life.

I don't advise anyone to have a three-day posterior labour, ending in an emergency C-section, but if you are going to have one, it's good to know it's really not a wasted event.

A Good Birth

Two and a half years later, I'm doing it all over again. I've put a baby inside me and allowed its head to grow to a scarily large size. Now I have to go through the whole dilation thing again.

This time around, though, I'm doing things in another way. For starters, I haven't spent the last two months of my pregnancy thinking, Let Christmas last for ever! Every morning can start with two mince pies, served with cream, six Miniature Heroes and some Pringles! As a result, I haven't put on three stone, and I can do things like 'walking', 'standing' and 'getting off the sofa without making an Oooof! sound'.

I have been to all my birth classes. It's taken me until I'm twenty-seven years old, but I now believe that a cervix really is a hole. And this time I know something that I just didn't before: it's not going to kill me. Now I know how birth works, I feel I've finally been told what my task is. It's simple – so simple I'm amazed I didn't know it before.

One morning I am going to wake up, and before I sleep again, I will have to tick off a long list of contractions, one by one. And when I get to the last one, I will have my girl. Each one of these will be a job in itself – a minute-long event which would alarm anyone suddenly struck by it, without warning – but I know the one fact that makes it easy: there is nothing wrong. Everything is as it should be. Unlike all other pain on earth, these don't signal something going wrong but something going right.

This is what I did not realise the first time, when I prayed wildly for the pains to stop. Then, I didn't know that these pains were actually the answer. Now I know what they are, and what they're for, I greet each one with calm cheer: sixty seconds to breathe through, as limp as a sleeping child.

By the time I get to the hospital, I'm contracting so hard that I drop to my knees in the doorway with much drama, and clutch at the nearest object – a life-size statue of the Virgin Mary. Four nurses have to run to stop it toppling over and crushing me. For this birth, I don't lie on a bed, helpless – waiting for a baby to be delivered, by room service. I've been told to walk, and I do – I pace miles and miles. I use the hospital corridors like the world's slowest, fattest racetrack. I walk for four hours, non-stop. Oh Nancy! I walk from St Paul's to Hammersmith for you, barefoot, quietly sighing, from Angel to Oval, the Palace to the Heath. Your head is like stone against bone – a quiet pressure I can't stop now, and neither can you.

Gravity is the magic I couldn't find before, strapped to the bed, two years ago. Gravity was the spell I should have called on. I was looking in all the wrong places.

After four hours of pacing, everything changes, and I know I have walked far enough. I climb into the pool, and push Nancy out in five short bursts. As her face appears, even I can see it's too late to go wrong now.

'That was easy!' I shout, the first words out of my mouth, before she has even left the water, as the midwives stand by with towels, waiting to wrap her. 'That was easy! Why doesn't anyone tell you it's so easy!'

Chapter 9

Why You Shouldn't Have Children

Of course, having children is hard work. A minimum eighteen-year task at full throttle, followed by another forty years of part-time fretting and money lending. And getting on their nerves when you keep cutting their toast into soldiers – even though they're now thirty-eight, and a surgeon. But in many ways, it's the easy option for a woman.

Why? Because, if you have children, at least people won't keep asking you when you're going to have children. For some reason, the world really wants to know when women are having children. It likes them to have planned this shit early. It wants them to be very clear and upfront about it – 'Oh, I'd like a glass of Merlot, the clams, the steak – and a baby when I'm thirty-two, please.'

And if a woman should say she doesn't want to have children at all, the world is apt to go highly peculiar. 'Ooooh, don't speak too soon,' it will say. Or 'When you meet the right man, you'll change your mind, dear.'

It is presumed that women will always end up having babies. They might go through silly phases of pretending that it's something that they have no interest in. But, when push comes to shove, womanhood is a cul-de-sac that ends in Mothercare, and that's the end of that. All women love babies – just like all women love shoes, and George Clooney. Even the ones who wear nothing but trainers, and really hate shoes, and George Clooney.

So, really, you're kind of helping them when you ask them when they're going to finally get on with it, and have a baby. But when women are asked when they're going to have children, there is really another, darker question lying beneath it. If you listen very, very carefully you can hear it.

It's this: 'When are you going to fuck it all up by having kids?' When are you going to blow a four-year chunk, minimum, out of your career by having a baby? When are you going to put all your creative talent and power on hold, in order to tend to the helpless, minute-by-minute needs of your newly born?

When are you going to stop making films/ albums/ books/deals? When do the holes start appearing in your CV? When do you get left behind, and forgotten? CAN WE GET POPCORN AND WATCH?

When people ask working women, 'When are you going to have a baby?' what they're really asking is, 'When are you going to leave?' And the question is always '*When* are you going to have kids?' Rather than 'Do you *want* to have kids?' Women are so often scared about their body clocks – 'YOU'VE ONLY GOT TWO YEARS LEFT TO HAVE A BABY!' – that they never get the chance to think if they actually care or not if the damn thing grinds to a halt.

With female fertility being seen as something limited, and due to vanish quite soon, there's a risk of women panicking and having a baby, 'just in case'. On the one hand, they didn't really want it, but on the other they might not have the chance to get one again, so better safe than sorry. It's not unknown for mothers to say at 2 a.m., and gin-truthful, 'It's not that I wish I hadn't had Chloe and Jack. It's just, if I could do it all again, I don't know whether I'd have kids at all.'

But deciding not to have children is a very, very hard decision for a woman to make.

Current thinking makes it hard to say, 'I choose not to,' or, 'It all sounds a bit vile, to be honest.' We call these women 'selfish'. The sense of the word 'childless' is of lack, and loss.

We think of non-mothers as rangy lone wolves – rattling around, as dangerous as teenage boys, or men. We make women feel that their stories have ground to a halt in their thirties if they don't have children and 'finish things' properly.

This call for all women to have children isn't logical. If you take a moment to look at the state of the world, the thing you notice is that there are plenty of babies being born. The planet really doesn't need all of us to produce more babies. Let's face it, most women will continue to have babies. The planet isn't going to run out of new people, so it's of no real use to the world for you to have a child.

Quite the opposite, in fact. That shouldn't stop you having one if you want one, of course. A cheery cry of 'Yes – but my baby might grow up to be JESUS. Or EINSTEIN! Or JESUS EINSTEIN!' is all the excuse you need, if you actually want one.

It's also worth keeping in mind that it's not of vital use to you as a woman . Yes, you could learn thousands of great things about love, strength, faith, fear, human relationships, blood ties and the effect of apricots on an immature digestive system. But I don't think there's a single lesson that motherhood has to offer that couldn't be learned elsewhere.

If you want to know what's in motherhood for you, as a woman, then – in truth – it's nothing you couldn't get from, say:

climbing hills
loving recklessly
sitting quietly, alone, in the dawn
drinking whisky with rebels
learning to do close-hand magic
swimming in a river in winter
growing foxgloves, peas and roses
calling your mum
singing while you walk
being polite
always, always helping strangers.

No one has ever claimed for a moment that childless men have missed out on a vital aspect of their lives, and were the poorer for it, or crippled by it. Every woman who chooses – joyfully, thoughtfully, calmly, of their own free will and desire – not to have a child, does womankind a massive favour in the long term.

We need more women who are allowed to prove their worth as people, rather than being judged merely for their chances of creating new people. After all, half those new people we go on to create are also women – presumably to be judged, in the future, for not making new people.

Feminism needs Zero Tolerance over baby angst. In the twenty-first century, it can't be about who we might make, and what they might do, any more. It has to be about who we are, and what we're going to do.

Chapter 10

Abortion

I've been to my GP three times with symptoms – acne, exhaustion, weight gain, odd menstrual cycle – and this is where they've referred me: the Ultrasound Unit at the Whittington Hospital.

Yes – with those symptoms, you think I'm pregnant, don't you? But I did a test six weeks ago: nothing. And so this is where my GP has sent me. I'm eating two cans of tinned pineapple for breakfast, and cry when I see a sad squirrel in an advert. Of course I'm pregnant. But the test said not. And I'm still breast-feeding. And I don't want to be pregnant. So I'm not.

As the nurse washes her hands, the ultrasound screen looks like the view from the deck of the Millennium Falcon in the *Star Wars* movies, when it's parked up. Dark, black space, with a few speckles of light. When they finally put the ultrasound to my belly, though, the whole solar system roars into life. And then, at the centre

– low, deep, hidden – a signal. A clock that's ticking. A heartbeat.

'You're pregnant!' the nurse says, cheerfully.

Nurses must be told to always say this cheerfully. They always do – however pale the client is, or however loudly the client has just said 'Fuck' and started shaking. She is doing sums, with an on-screen tape measure.

'I would say you're around eleven weeks,' she says, pushing the ultrasound screen into my belly.

That really is it – there is nothing else that looks like a foetus. The curve of the spine, like a crescent moon. The astronaut-helmet skull. The black, unblinking eyes, like a prawn.

'Oh my God,' I say, to the baby.

I am sure he is my gay son – the one I always wanted. His entrance is so showy – so jazz-hands, so 'Ta-da!' So sudden. So camp. Keep him a secret until he can appear like this, on TV; like it's fucking Parkinson or something.

And his luck! This kid is clearly lucky – we only had one unprotected fuck. That night in Cyprus, in the twenty minutes both girls were asleep. This kid is going to buck odds all his life: he'll break casinos, and make friends with millionaires in the deli queue. He'll find gold the first time he pans the stream, and true love on the very day he decides he needs to settle down.

'I can't have you,' I tell him, sadly. 'The world will fall in if I have you.'

Because not even for a second do I think I should have this baby. I have no dilemma, no terrible decision to make. I know, with calm certainty, that I don't want another child now, in the same way I know that I don't want to go to India, or be blonde, or fire a gun.

I thank the nurse, wipe the jelly from my stomach and go outside to make a call.

In 2007, *Guardian* columnist Zoe Williams wrote a wholly clear-headed piece about why women always felt they must begin talking about their abortions by saying, 'Of course, it's terribly traumatic. No woman enters into this lightly.'

Zoe Williams went on to explain that this is because, however liberal a society, it assumes that, at its core, abortion is wrong. But that a forgiving society must make it legal and provide for it medically. Otherwise desperate women might go down a back alley to 'do a Vera Drake', and make things even worse.

Abortions are never seen as a good thing. Women never speak publicly about their abortions by happily giving thanks. There are no

'Good luck with your morning-after pill!' cards. People don't make jokes about it, although all the truest jokes are about tricky topics and cover every other subject, including cancer, God and death.

Also, there is the spectrum of 'wrongness' to think about. There are 'good abortions' and 'bad abortions': a raped teenage girl seeking an abortion – or a mother whose life is put at risk by the pregnancy – is having a 'good' abortion. She still won't discuss it publicly, or expect her friends to be happy for her, but these women get away with barely any judgement.

At the other end of the spectrum, of course, are the 'worst' kind of abortions: repeated abortions, late-term abortions, abortions after IVF, and – worst of all – mothers who have abortions. Our view of motherhood is of someone perfect – Mother, gentle giver of life – making the thought of a mother refusing to give further life seems obscene.

But both science and philosophy still struggle to define what the beginning of 'life' is. Wouldn't it be better, then, to look at abortion from a different angle? If a pregnant woman has power over life, why should she not also have power over not-life? If women are led, by biology, to host, shelter, nurture and protect life, why should they not be able to end life, too?

My belief in the need for abortion became even stronger after I had my two children. It is only after you have had a nine-month pregnancy, laboured to get the child out, fed it, cared for it, sat with it until 3 a.m., risen with it at 6 a.m., swooned with love for it, and been moved to furious tears by it that you really understand just how important it is for a child to be wanted. And how motherhood is a game you must enter with as much energy, goodwill and happiness as possible. And the most important thing of all, of course, is to be wanted, desired and cared for by a reasonably sane, stable mother.

I can honestly say that my abortion was one of the least difficult decisions of my life. I'm not being flippant when I say it took me longer to decide what worktops to have in the kitchen. Because I knew that to do it again – to commit my life to another person – might very possibly stretch me to breaking point.

The idea that I might not – in an earlier era, or another country – have a choice in the matter, seems barbaric, both emotionally and physically. Women are often too ashamed, or too afraid of a reaction, to discuss their abortions, even with friends or partners. It is curious that, while pretty much everyone must have someone dear to them who has had an abortion, the chances of them actually discussing it with their more cautious elders, or menfolk, are remote.

So, we have a climate where anti-abortionists can discuss abortion as something that 'they' do, over 'there', rather than the reality – that it has, very likely, been a calm, rational, well-thought-out act, which has occurred very close to home.

When I wrote about my decision to have an abortion in *The Times*, I was amazed at the reader-response – more than 400 online comments, and over 100 letters and emails. It seemed that those who were anti-abortion mentioned no experience of pregnancy or abortion, while those who were pro-abortion did.

My first – wanted, so badly – ended in miscarriage, three days before my wedding. A kind nurse removed my wedding manicure with nail-polish remover, in order to fit a finger-thermometer for the subsequent operation on my womb. I wept as I went into the operating theatre and wept as I came out.

In that instance, my body had decided that this baby was not to be and had ended it. This time, it is my mind that has decided that this baby is not to be. I don't believe one decision is more valid than the other. They both know me. They are both equally able to decide what is right.

In the waiting room of the clinic we go to, there are four couples, and two women on their own. The younger woman is from Ireland – she arrived here this morning, and – I gather, from what she is whispering to the receptionist – will go back on the ferry tonight. The older woman looks in her late forties, maybe even early fifties. She cries without making a sound. She has the air of a woman who hasn't told a soul, and never will. The couples are silent, too – all possible words have been said, before you get here.

The nurse calls my name.

I don't know what I thought abortion would be like. When I went into surgery after my miscarriage, they knocked me out – weeping – and I woke up – weeping – with it all over.

This time, I'm awake for all of it. The whole thing is a bad surprise. I suppose I thought the one thing it would be was 'clinical' – doctors just doing their job, coldly and quickly; their actions precise and fast. But as I lie on the bed – the last appointment of the day – the doctors have the air of people who've spent far too long doing unpleasant things, correcting the mistakes of others. It's quite painful – like labour, five hours in.

The painkiller has been useless, but complaining about pain, given what you are doing, seems wrong. Even if you don't believe you should suffer pain while having an abortion, there's a feeling in the air that the staff here do.

'You're doing fine,' the nurse says, holding my hand hard. She is kind, but she is also, obviously, already putting her coat on, and thinking about getting out the door. She can smell the weekend from here. She is already far away.

The doctor then uses a small machine called a 'vacurette' to hoover my womb out, which is pretty much exactly as you'd imagine having the contents of your womb vacuumed out to feel like. In the months after, I pull back more than once from buying a Black & Decker Dustbuster.

The whole process has taken maybe seven minutes – it is brisk – but the longing for every instrument and hand to retreat from you, and allow you to knit quietly back together, and heal, is immense. You want everyone to GET OUT of you. Everyone. The doctor turns the vacuum off. He then turns it on again, and does one last little bit: like when you're doing the front room, finish, and then decide to give the sofa cushions a once-over, while you're at it.

Finally, he's done, and I let out an unplanned 'Ahhh!' as his hand withdraws.

'See!' he says, with a firm smile. 'Not too bad! All done!' Then he looks down into the dish, which holds everything that was inside me. Seeing something, he calls his colleague over, from the sluice. 'Look at that!' he says, pointing.

'Hahaha – unusual!' the other says.

They both laugh, before the dish is carried away, and the gloves are peeled off, and the cleaning up starts. The day is now done.

When they take you into the next room – the 'Recovery Room' – you lie, wrapped in a towelling robe, on a reclining chair. They give you a magazine, and a cold drink. There is a potted palm tree in the corner. It looks like the worst-ever re-make of Wham!'s 'Club Tropicana' video.

The girl from Ireland leaves after five minutes – she has to catch her bus, to catch her coach, to catch her ferry back home. She walks sore. It's obvious that she shouldn't have had to come to another country to get her life back on track.

I wonder if the judges in Ireland have ever seen a woman as pale as this, counting out fifty pound notes onto the reception desk in a country where she doesn't know a soul. And then bleeding all the way from Essex to Holyhead. I wonder if her father approves of the law because he doesn't think it applies to her – and whether he would hate that law if he knew it did.

The older woman – who was crying, silently, in the waiting room – is here too. None of us looks at each other. We just read the magazines until the forty minutes' 'recovery time' is up, and the nurse says, 'You can go.'

And we drive away – with my husband driving dangerously, because he's holding my hand very, very tight – and I say, 'I'm going to get the contraceptive version of Trident fitted, I think.' And he says, 'Yeah,' and holds my hand even tighter. And that is the end of that day.

Given the subject matter, it seems odd to say that this is the happy ending – but it is. All stories of abortion seem to have a sad ending, how the process left a mark. However friendly to women the writer is, there is a need to mention how the day of the abortion is always remembered with sorrow – and the baby's due date marked with a sudden flood of tears.

The story is that while a woman may tell herself, rationally, that she couldn't have that baby, there will be a part of her that does not believe this. A part of her carries on silently marking the baby that should have come. Women's bodies do not give up their babies so easily, and so silently, is the message. The heart will always remember.

This is what I expect. But this is not how it is. Indeed, it's the opposite. I keep waiting for my grief and guilt to come. I am braced, chest out, ready – but it never arrives. I don't cry when I see baby clothes. Friends being pregnant don't make me jealous, or quietly blue.

I do not have to remind myself that sometimes, you must do the 'wrong' thing for the 'right' reason. In fact, it's the opposite. Every time I sleep through the night, I am thankful for the choice I made. When the youngest stops wearing nappies, I'm pleased there isn't a third one, following behind.

When friends come round with their new babies, I am hugely, hugely grateful that I had the option not to do this again. And I'm pleased that the option, my abortion, didn't involve me lying on a friend's kitchen table, after the kids had gone to sleep, praying I wouldn't get an infection, or bleed to death before I got home.

I suppose what I'd been led to believe is that my body – or my subconscious mind – would be angry with me for not having the baby. But all I could see – and all I can see now, years later – is history filled with millions of women trying to undo the mistake that could then undo them. And then those women just carrying on, quiet, thankful and silent about the whole thing. What I see, is that it really can be an action with only good results.

Postscript

London, October 2020

So do I know how to be a woman now?

The easy thing would be to say, 'No. No, I still don't have a clue! I'm just still the same well-meaning idiot I was at thirteen. I'm still just a chimp in a frock with a laptop, setting fire to saucepans, falling down staircases, saying the wrong thing and feeling like a nervous child inside. I'm a buffoon! A div! A numnut!'

Because, of course, there are still ways in which I don't know how to be a woman yet. I have not had to deal with family bereavement, or the menopause, or losing my job. I still can't iron, do maths, drive a car or – and I must be frank here – 100 per cent reliably remember which is 'left' and which is 'right' in an emergency.

There are still a million things I have left to learn. A billion. A trillion. In terms of how much better I could be, I've barely even been born yet. I'm still an *egg*.

But then, on the other hand, I distrust this female habit of blindly flagging up your own flaws. I don't mean the breezy, airy, witty remark in the face of a compliment – 'Lost weight? No. We're just in a larger room than usual, darling.' 'You think my children are well mannered? I have wired them with small electrodes, and every time they misbehave, I punch the "Bad Kid" button in my pocket.' That's fine.

No – I'm talking about the common habit in women that we're kind of . . . failing if we're not a bit troubled. That we're somehow boorish, complacent and unfeminine if we're content. So, if I was asked, 'Do you know how to be a woman now?', my answer would be, 'Kind of *yes*, really, to be honest.'

Because if all the stories in this book add up to one single revelation, it is this: to just . . . not really give a shit about all that stuff. To not care about all those supposed 'problems' of being a woman. To refuse to see them as problems at all.

Yes – when I had my massive feminist awakening, the action it caused in me was a . . . big shrug. As it turned out, almost every idea I had on my thirteenth birthday about my future turned out to be a total waste of my time. When I thought of myself as an adult, all I could imagine was someone thin, and smooth, and calm, to whom things ... happened.

I didn't have any idea about improving myself, or following my interests, or learning big life lessons, or, most importantly, finding out what I was good at, and trying to earn a living from it. I presumed that some grown-ups would come along and basically tell me all these things, tell me what to do, at some point, and that I shouldn't really worry about them. I didn't worry about what I was going to do.

What I did worry about, and thought I should work hard at, was what I should *be*, instead. I thought all my efforts should be focused on *being* fabulous, rather than *doing* fabulous things. I thought that once I'd cracked being thin, beautiful, stylishly dressed, poised and gracious, everything else would fall into place. That my real life's work was not a career – but myself. That if I worked on being pleasing, the world would adore, and then reward me.

When I think of everything that crippled me with fear about 'being a woman' when I was thirteen, it all came down, really, to 'being a princess'. I didn't think I'd have to work hard to become a woman – which is scary but, obviously, in the end can be done. Instead, I thought things would happen to me, just because I was 'enchanting'. That's how I'd get fallen in love with. That's how I'd make my way in the world.

But if I could tell you the one thing that has given me the most freedom and relief in my adult years, it's finally giving up, once and for all, any idea that I would one day become a princess. Here's all the ways I now know I am *not* a princess.

1) I can't sing. Admitting that to myself was a massive sorrow. All princesses sing. All women are supposed to be able to sing. They can make birds be their friends, as soon as they start trilling. I, on the other hand, sound like the noise gigantic eighteen-wheeler trucks make, just before they crash into a police roadblock. HONK HONK. SCREECH. 'Oh my God – *no one* will come out of *that* alive!'

2) I don't taste sweet – like cake, or honey. I can't tell you the number of filthy books I've read that led me to believe that, when a man went down on you, he was basically munching away on a bag of Haribo. The first time someone commented – positively, mind you – that I tasted like 'a lovely pie', I cried for two hours afterwards. What kind of stompy, sweaty item was I? Was I a hog

roast? But we are, of course, sweaty, fleshy lady-animals. Of *course* we don't taste like trifle – *like a princess would.*

3) I'm not ever going to be worshipped by some powerful, rich, sword-wielding man who will change my life. Because those guys literally don't exist. Have you *ever* met one? No. I don't *want* some brutal, alpha beast. And actually, I don't know *anyone* who wants one.

What all my lady friends want, instead, is some geeky, nerdy, polite and ridiculous mate who we can sit at home with, slagging off all the tossers, and waiting for our baked potatoes to be ready. Who, obviously, is also so hot for us that they often crawl across the front room floor, croaking, 'I must have sex with you now, or go literally insane.' Compared to that sweet dude, Prince Charming looks like a total donk.

4) Princesses never have a gang. They never have any mates. There's no palling around. Princesses never sit outside a pub with their best friends on a crisp autumn afternoon, putting their favourite Beatles records in chart order. Princesses are *lonely*. I'm not a princess. I'm not a princess! I'm a honking, sweaty, hard-working lady who loves her geeky husband and funny mates. And it's *brilliant*.

Simply being honest about who we really are is half the battle. You know what – <u>if what you read in magazines and papers and online makes you feel uneasy or shitty – don't read it!</u> If you feel panicky at the idea of an expensive wedding – ignore your mother-in-law, run away to a registry office!

And if you think a £600 handbag is obscene, instead of bravely saying, 'I'll just have to max my credit card,' just say, 'Actually, I can't afford it.' There's so much stuff – in every respect – that we can't afford, and yet we let ourselves go for, in order to join in, and feel 'normal'.

But, of course, if everyone is too anxious to say what their real position is, then there is a new, communal, middling experience, which is being kept secret by everyone being too embarrassed to say, 'Don't think I'm a freak, but ...'

Feminism is being truthful about what it's *truly* like to be a woman, and then talking about how we could make it *better*. It's not as if this would only be good for women: for if equality for women truly comes to pass – as the slow, unstoppable gravity of social and economic change suggests it must – then it's going to work out pretty peachy for the men too.

If I were the ruling men I would be *thrilled* at the idea of women finally getting an equal crack of the whip. Let's face it – the ruling men must be knackered by now. It's been 40,000 years without even so much as a tea break: men have been flat out ruling the world. They have been balls to the wall.

Faced, then, with the option of some manner of shared time – women ruling the world half the time – the ruling men could finally take their feet off the gas a bit. Go on that holiday they've been talking about for years; really sort the shed out, once and for all. The ruling men could get stuck into some hardcore paintballing weekends.

Because it's not as if strident feminists want to take over from men. We're not looking for the whole world. Just *our share*. The men don't really have to change a thing. As far as I'm concerned, men can just carry on doing pretty much whatever they like. I don't want men to go away. I don't want men to stop what they're doing. What I want, instead, are some radical market forces. I want CHOICE. I want VARIETY. I want MORE. I want WOMEN. I want women to have more of the world, not just because it would be fairer, but because it would be better. More exciting. Re-ordered. Re-invented.

We should have the lady-balls to say, 'Yeah – I like the look of this world. And I've been here for a good while, watching. Now – here's how I'd tweak it. Because we're all in this together. We're all just, you know. The Guys.'

So, in the end, I suppose the title of the book isn't quite right. All through those stumbling, embarrassing, amazing years, I thought that what I wanted to be was a woman. To be some incredible blend of Germaine Greer, Elizabeth Taylor, Courtney Love, Jilly Cooper and Lady Gaga. To find some way of mastering all the strange arts of being female, until I was some perfect form of all the things that confused and defeated me at the outset, in my bed, in Wolverhampton, at the age of thirteen. A princess. A goddess. A muse.

But as the years went on, I realised that what I really want to be, all told, is a human. Just a productive, honest, warmly treated human. One of 'The Guys'.

But with really amazing hair.

About Quick Reads

"Reading is such an important building block for success"
- Jojo Moyes

Quick Reads are short books written by best-selling authors. They are perfect for regular readers and those who are still to discover the pleasure of reading.

Did you enjoy this Quick Read?
Tell us what you thought by filling in our short survey. Scan the QR code to go directly to the survey or visit
https://bit.ly/QuickReads2021

Turn over to find your next Quick Read…

A special thank you to Jojo Moyes for her generous donation and support of Quick Reads and to Here Design.

Quick Reads is part of The Reading Agency, a national charity tackling life's big challenges through the proven power of reading.

www.readingagency.org.uk
@readingagency   #QuickReads

The Reading Agency Ltd. Registered number: 3904882 (England & Wales)
Registered charity number: 1085443 (England & Wales)
Registered Office: Free Word Centre, 60 Farringdon Road, London, EC1R 3GA
The Reading Agency is supported using public funding by Arts Council England.

Supported using public funding by
**ARTS COUNCIL
ENGLAND**

THE READING AGENCY

Find your next Quick Read: the 2021 series

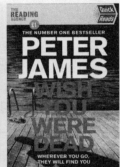

Available to buy in paperback or ebook and to borrow from your local library.

More from Quick Reads

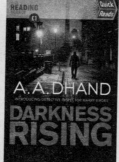

For a complete list of titles and more information on the authors and their books visit

www.readingagency.org.uk/quickreads

Continue your reading journey

The Reading Agency is here to help keep you and your family reading:

Challenge yourself to complete six reads
by taking part in Reading Ahead
at your local library, college or workplace
readingahead.org.uk

Join Reading Groups for Everyone to find a
reading group and discover new books
readinggroups.org.uk

Celebrate reading on World Book Night
every year on 23 April
worldbooknight.org

Read with your family as part of the
Summer Reading Challenge
at your local library
summerreadingchallenge.org.uk

For more information, please visit our website:
readingagency.org.uk

If you enjoyed *How To Be A Woman*, you will love *How To Build A Girl*, Caitlin Moran's number one bestselling novel, and now a major feature film.

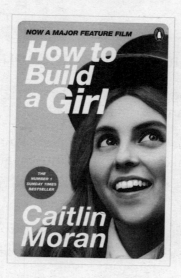

My name's Johanna Morrigan. I'm fourteen, and I've just decided to kill myself.

I don't really want to die, of course! I just need to kill Johanna, and build a new girl. Dolly Wilde will be everything I want to be, and more! But as with all the best coming-of-age stories, it doesn't exactly go to plan . . .

A Number One *Sunday Times* bestseller, *How To Build A Girl* is the hilarious novel from Caitlin Moran.

'Brilliantly observed, thrillingly rude and laugh-out-loud funny'
Helen Fielding

'Binge-read all of #HowToBuildAGirl in one sitting. Even missed supper'
Nigella Lawson

'A riotous read with jokes galore cut through with lightly handled serious observations about the nature of poverty and the challenges of emerging female sexuality'
Sunday Times

How To Be Famous: the hilarious, bestselling
sequel to *How To Build A Girl*

I'm **Johanna Morrigan**, and I live in London in 1995, at the epicentre
of Britpop. I might only be nineteen, but I'm wise enough to know that
everyone around me is handling fame very, very badly.

My unrequited love, **John Kite**, has scored an unexpected Number One
album, then exploded into a Booze And Drugs Hell™ – as rockstars
do. And my new best friend – the maverick feminist **Suzanne Banks,
of The Branks** – has amazing hair, but writer's block and a rampant pill
problem. So I've decided I should become a **Fame Doctor**. I'm going to
use my new monthly column for *The Face* to write about every ridiculous,
surreal, amazing aspect of a million people knowing your name.

But when my two-night-stand with edgy comedian **Jerry Sharp** goes
wrong, people start to know *my* name for all the wrong reasons. 'He's a
vampire. He destroys bright young girls. Also, he's a total dick' Suzanne
warned me. But by that point, I'd already had sex with him. Bad sex.

Now I'm one of the girls he's trying to destroy.

He needs to be stopped.

But how can one woman stop a bad, famous, powerful man?